# The World in My Mouth

Josef Tomáš

Published 2009 by arima publishing
www.arimapublishing.com

ISBN 978-1-84549-382-0

© Josef Tomáš, 2009
First appeared in Czech as *Svět v ústech*, published by Carpe Diem in 2001
Translated by the author and Katarina Tomas

© Cover by Virginia MacKenny: *Subatomic Particles Trace*, oil on acrylic on canvas, detail (70cmx70cm) from the painting installation *Sleepers (sightlines)*, 2001-2003

All rights reserved

This book is copyright. Subject to statutory exception and to provisions of relevant collective licensing agreements, no part of this publication may be reproduced, stored in a retrieval system, or transmitted in any form or by any means, without the prior written permission of the author.

Printed and bound in the United Kingdom

Typeset in Palatino 12/16

This book is sold subject to the conditions that it shall not, by way of trade or otherwise, be lent, re-sold, hired out, or otherwise circulated without the publisher's prior consent in any form of binding or cover other than that which it is published and without a similar condition including this condition being imposed on the subsequent purchaser.

arima publishing
ASK House, Northgate Avenue
Bury St Edmunds, Suffolk IP32 6BB
t: (+44) 01284 700321
www.arimapublishing.com

*Dedicated to Dr. Paul Davies*

# Contents

| | |
|---|---|
| The Poetry of Nature | 7 |
| The nutcracker | 9 |
| The weight of life | 10 |
| Really nothing | 11 |
| Friday is here again | 12 |
| A spark of life | 13 |
| Fragmentation | 14 |
| Fantasy | 15 |
| There is no way out | 16 |
| Sunflowers | 17 |
| Promises, just promises | 18 |
| Mathematics | 19 |
| A short day | 20 |
| A little pea | 21 |
| The strength of breath | 22 |
| Heaviness of a day | 23 |
| Alzheimer's | 24 |
| Buddha's finger | 25 |
| A cellar full of junk | 26 |
| A razor's edge | 27 |
| Space | 28 |
| Life | 29 |
| That mystery | 30 |
| The world | 31 |
| Silence | 32 |

| | |
|---|---:|
| Milarepa's carious tooth | 33 |
| Emptiness and life | 34 |
| The mind | 35 |
| Stupefaction | 36 |
| Houses on the hillside | 37 |
| The table of cave men | 38 |
| Noise | 39 |
| Everywhere only Man | 40 |
| Trees in the wind | 41 |
| Our heads | 42 |
| Everything and nothing | 43 |
| Things on sale | 44 |
| Motion | 45 |
| Gravitation | 46 |
| A cathedral | 47 |
| Distance | 48 |
| The Milky Way | 49 |
| The afterglow | 50 |
| Paul Davies | 51 |
| Virginia MacKenny | 52 |
| Josef Tomáš | 54 |

# The Poetry of Nature

From **The Big Questions**, *Paul Davies in conversation with Phillip Adams*; presented by the ABC in 1995 as a six-part series, filmed at Cooper Pedy in the Australian Outback.

**Phillip**: Are you suggesting that mathematics may be a universal language?

**Paul**: Yes, I am. You see, the laws of nature are mathematical in form. The great book of nature, remarked Galileo, is written in mathematical language. Any species of intelligent beings out there that has developed technology is going to be familiar with the basic mathematical laws of the universe. So that will be the starting point of any dialogue.

**Phillip**: Paul, you realise that the universal language you speak so fluently is unavailable to many others. I don't speak it and our film crew doesn't either. You are the only person in this remote location who does. I suppose we should take comfort in the thought of you being able to communicate with another species, even if you can't communicate with many of your fellow human beings!

**Paul**: One of the great tragedies in trying to explain basic physics and cosmology, indeed any science, to the general public is that most people are afraid of mathematics. They don't like and they don't know much of it, and consequently they are shut off from the language and the poetry of nature.

---

"The Big Questions – The Creative Cosmos" first published in 2002 and reproduced by permission of the Australian Broadcasting Corporation and ABC Online. © 2002 All rights reserved. The full transcript is available at:
http://www.abc.net.au/science/bigquestions/s459858.htm

## The nutcracker

Oh, what a delight to learn how to reveal
the world. To harvest it like hazelnuts,
from the fabled gardens of space,
and crack it open in my hungry mouth.

But do not forget what they truly are:
in space but dust, yet falling stars for me,
revealed by the traces they were forced to make
in order to change from nothing into something.

*Josef Tomáš*

## The weight of life

Oh, how loaded, and leaden, and laden
is life – with many petty pitfalls
and a few unbearable sufferings,
piled upon us – by us.

By day, all is like salt in water:
dissolved and unseen – but at night:
the sharp edges of those growing crystals
cut into our unhealed wounds.

## Really nothing

Oh, how frail and vulnerable our Earth appears
to be. A godforsaken blue-white ball
suspended high in the fathomless void
of space ... How then are we not to despair?

It must be the angelic drapery,
sewn from the azure blue of the sky,
that shields us from seeing that nothing is there,
for zillions of miles nothing ... nothing ...

*Josef Tomáš*

## Friday is here again

Oh you, my time! – you are always racing
away from me. Is it really Friday again? –
Did not the last one end just yesterday,
with the whole week still ahead of me?

How can I slow you down, if you can't be stopped?
Would it help if I caressed what I touched,
not just with my hands, but also with my mind? –
And for a while longer than I have done up to now?
  – Maybe …

## A spark of life

Oh, how impossible it is for us
to comprehend death. We recall so much,
but there is still more to come, and yet –
tomorrow already – it all may end.

Can some relief be found in the thought
that all will remain as it has always been?
Thus nothing ahead and nothing behind,
just two black flints that sparked the fire of life …

*Josef Tomáš*

## Fragmentation

Oh, how fragmented everything is,
both around and inside of us. As if, eons ago,
God exploded and was dispersed
in countless splinters, near and far.

We are but fragments of God torn asunder.
Endlessly he's been surging with his void:
merging, binding until in a few grains
He awoke and became conscious in us.

## Fantasy

Oh, how powerful is the fantasy
of the human mind; with no restrictions at all.
No wonder one feels more at home elsewhere
and at some other time than here and now.

But were it not for the *here and now* of the body,
reality would evaporate like water from a pot,
and at the bottom of our empty heads
only a few fossilized dreams would remain.

*Josef Tomáš*

## There is no way out

Oh, what sowers and reapers of fate
we are! One word here, one word there, and soon
many heads will sprout a small crop
that, by and large, turns out to be just useless
     weeds.

And there is no way out. Simply *being*
predestines us to intrude upon others.
Even if we were to vanish,
like ghosts we would keep haunting them.

## Sunflowers

Oh you, a field of sunflowers in bloom
that brighten my life! I only have to look
at your flowers, and they instantly seem to turn
their heads towards me, as if *I* were the sun.

Is it because millions of your sisters
also gleam inside of me,
reflecting the sun? ... So, be it inside or outside,
everywhere life is in full bloom.

*Josef Tomáš*

## Promises, just promises

Oh, how much I have promised everyone –
and myself the most. Others know me
far too well to believe what I say,
but have I learned so little about myself?

For all those nights and days I have been alive,
how have I managed, time and time again,
to convince myself that by tomorrow
I can change into someone else?

## Mathematics

Oh you, the rigorously stringent quintessence
of mathematics, sister of music and poetry!
Depersonalization is required from each of you,
if reality is to be credibly reflected.

In symbols only – be it numbers, sounds or words –
can the inexplicable be expressed. A mere hint
of a discovery excites me like a gambler
who comes within reach of a sudden win.

*Josef Tomáš*

## A short day

Oh, how terribly short a day
can appear. And, the more it seems shortened,
the more the night seems stretched out
by awakening, insomnia, vigilance.

Shortly after midnight, it is always dark,
be it winter or summer. One should then be
deeply asleep – not, half-sitting, half-lying,
scribbling down the words of a pointless poem.

## A little pea

Oh, how are we to comprehend the innumerability
of everything. How does it go again? First, the
> number *one*,

followed by *twenty-four zeros* – this being
the number of atoms inside one miniscule pea.

If each one was a dot, spaced twelve per inch
and two miles high, all of France would be filled.
And it is also more than the sum of all letters
in every book ever printed … Oh, what wonder!

*Josef Tomáš*

## The strength of breath

Oh you, the unrecognized strength
of breath! You have become so obvious, so clear,
since I have calmed my restlessness and now
only feel the air streaming in and out …

Slowly, the indistinctive sea of space swells
with dazzling waves and I, full of wonder,
exclaim: "Oh, what I've seen so far was only
the lining of a most exquisitely dressed world!"

## Heaviness of a day

Oh, how hard it is sometimes to survive
even for just one day. From where do I accumulate
so many worries, when the nights
unburden me with pellucid dreams?

So many duties and necessities await me –
like a queue of claimants at a service counter.
How to satisfy them fully and on time?
How to arrive at just one worriless evening?

*Josef Tomáš*

## Alzheimer's

Oh, Babette! From where could you have caught
your Alzheimer's disease? I know
that it is not catching … could it have seeped
from an unknown, uncharted side of you?

Another side of you? And I had no idea
what was going on, and wondered how you could
  forget
that I was coming to stay. Oh, my ill-fated Babette,
with your soul caught between the two sides of you.

## Buddha's finger

Oh, how naive it is to seek assurance
from outside. Is it an inborn weakness
that forces us to rely upon others?
But how does that saying of Buddha's go?

"Why are you grasping my finger,
when it is the direction that I am pointing to?"
A direction where to? ... Inside? Outside? Or
towards a completely different *where*?

*Josef Tomáš*

## A cellar full of junk

Oh, how strange is my whole existence.
So much is happening inside of me, and yet
most of the time without me being present at all.
What is it, then, that I call *I*?

A helter-skelter of everything and anything.
A cellar full of junk, even though
the house looks tidy. But, for heaven's sake,
don't let anybody look under the carpet!

## A razor's edge

Oh you, the elusive and fleeting sense
of time! As soon as you appear,
you immediately disappear, and I cannot
hear you, nor see you or smell you.

Are you happening outside me at all?
From dreams to recollections, from plans to
    disappointments,
and in-between, narrower than a razor's edge, flows
    the present …
Is it any wonder that I cannot stay in it?

*Josef Tomáš*

## Space

Oh, how immeasurably fathomless is
space. And yet, if I catch sight of it
in two opposing mirrors, I see only myself,
and in countless copies at that.

Could space, like time, be fully contained
within me? This would explain why,
when I sometimes forget myself,
I feel at home everywhere.

## Life

Oh, how intricate beyond belief is
life. And yet, like the barely visible top
of a melting iceberg, it is kept afloat
by the accretion of submerged lifelessness.

I live, therefore I think I am.
And yet, everything here is truly nothing
but a dream kept alive
by the illusion of life's endlessness.

*Josef Tomáš*

## That mystery

Oh yes, it reverberates, it resounds –
that mystery in which, since time immemorial,
everything has been immersed.
It is boundless and has no name.

It must be shy beyond belief, because
when called by a name, it disappears …
And yet, it permeates everything –
that nameless mysterious something.

## The world

Oh, how unappeasable is our yearning to discern
the world. To uncover how everything works,
and how the unrestrained procreation of nothing
succeeded in creating so much of everything.

Look, how even the most miniscule thing conceals
a self-contained world! If only we knew
how to decipher it, and then – in wonder –
contemplate its overcrowded nothingness.

## Silence

Oh, how rich beyond any measure is
silence. And the more silent, the more
it points to an emptiness that –
inward and outward – fills everything.

We still can't grasp how we came
to be here. But, at least some of us
have succeeded in lessening their fear
of the unfathomable emptiness in everything.

## Milarepa's carious tooth

Oh, how vexing is the incessant care
of our bodies. And it can't be brushed aside,
that attention, day after day demanding:
"How do I look? How is my breath? Any pain here
 or there?"

I ponder what the Tibetan Milarepa might have
 done
when, for example, one of his teeth began to throb.
The smell of a rotting tooth can be ignored in a cave,
but the pain, before a carious tooth rots out? – !

## Emptiness and life

Oh, how fascinated I am, again and again,
by emptiness. And even more – by the dash of dust
it contains. How did it manage to compact,
fuse and, in the end, bring itself to life,

when every grain of dust contains
nothing but emptiness? How then –
on a lifeless crust of nothing –
can something exist that is so alive?

## The mind

Oh, how multifariously malleable is
my mind. As if it were made from moistened clay
and my will could form or deform it,
depending on my mood at a given moment.

I am provided with all I need:
a kick wheel, a lump of clay and, from time to time,
even potter's hands, when my craftsman-fate
takes a fancy and allows me to shape my life.

*Josef Tomáš*

## Stupefaction

Oh, is this a premonition of the end?
A sudden arrest of my body into torpidity,
my mind fossilized into apathy,
refusing to continue a meaningless life.

All at once, the present spreads wide
and stifles my movements and thoughts:
then all pain and joy disappear and I am left
lingering in a benumbed body …

## Houses on the hillside

Oh you, the incommunicative fronts of houses
on a hillside! Your doors are muted mouths,
and your windows blind eyes, mirroring the sky,
grey or blue, like the shifting moods of the weather.

And the people? – nowhere. As if they had
never been here and could not build anything,
and these houses stand on a hillside only
to mirror the changing moods of the weather.

*Josef Tomáš*

## The table of cave men

Oh, how every object here speaks to me
about its history. Take, for example, this table –
smooth and shiny, and its form! – what a joy
to look at, to take a seat and exchange a few words,

perhaps about the thoughts and hands that
 created it,
and passed it down from their rough ancestors
to this restaurant, where the descendants of
 cave men
strive (by the force of *their* thoughts) to appear
 civilized.

## Noise

Oh, how impossible it is to dodge
noise. At every step a cacophony of voices
intrudes upon us with the compelling belief
that we should feel lost without them.

One can understand that youngsters perhaps
 believe
it is so: when we were young, we also indulged
in naiveties. But to push it on us, who, so to speak,
are with one leg in the grave? – What insolence!

*Josef Tomáš*

## Everywhere only Man

Oh, show me something that does not conceal
Man, be it good or bad or good-for-nothing.
Always in a hurry, he never thinks
of what may come from all his doing.

So far, everything has turned out well:
scorched lands have re-grown, dead rivers have
 revived,
only a few kinds of plants, beasts and men
have died out, when they no longer could keep
 abreast of him.

## Trees in the wind

Oh, how fascinated I am by eucalyptus trees
swaying in the wind. Seen from a distance,
their tree-tops move majestically
and in tune with their lofty trunks.

Up close, however, each tuft of leaves
quivers like a cluster of errant bees
clutching to an upright stem, which,
though not seen, holds all of them together.

*Josef Tomáš*

## Our heads

Oh, what a multitude of things we see
in a single day! How can there be enough room
in us when so many relics fill our heads,
and there is still more to come.

Our heads are like kaleidoscopes:
they, too, rattle colourful shapes around
into tessellated pictures – from what has been
into what will never be, and never was.

## Everything and nothing

Oh, how amazed I am by everything.
Around me, inside me, everywhere by everything.
There is no need for miracles when everything
is beyond my imagination – everything!

Multiplied by zero (and thus nothing)
is the extent of my perception. And the same
      nothing
enfolds my comprehension. So, less than nothing
is my effort to comprehend everything in nothing.

*Josef Tomáš*

## Things on sale

Oh, what an abundance of things is
on sale. And every day there's more –
as if an inescapable law of nature necessitates
that what people produce must also become
> countless.

So, when one day everything has been processed,
and everything has been imported and exported,
and when even the last article has been sold,
then the indisputable end of the world will have
> arrived.

## Motion

Oh, like everything in life, the same mystery
enshrouds motion … Look at my hand here,
resting like an inanimate thing on this desk.
(But do not forget its reflection in your mind!)

Observe how I move it a little to one side.
The hand-object is still here; the hand-perception
    too.
But where is the hand from before? Only in your
    mind.
So, without your head, nothing can be moved.

*Josef Tomáš*

## Gravitation

Oh, how mysterious, because it is still unexplained,
is gravitation. And it fuses together not only dead
    matter.
Even words are merged into sentences or verses,
despite deceiving more than telling the truth.

All that is scattered is mutually attracted –
be it an object or a man, a thought or a word.
Nothing can evade the mystery
of all-pervasive gravitation.

## A cathedral

Oh, how the cathedral in my mind differs
from the one in a eulogy for a dead poet:
"At the time when fish will swim in cathedrals,
this poet will be called on by his name."

I have read that if an atom were a cathedral, its
 nucleus
would be a pearl, from the torn necklace of a
 princess,
that rolled into a crevice between two tiles. I
 exclaimed:
"My God, let nobody find it!" – but it was too late …

## Distance

Oh, it is better not to think about
the distance between us and the nearest star.
And it is, anyway, beyond our imagination;
only children manage to play with it:

*Alfa Beta Proxima*
*Centaur with three spying eyes*
*The Sun – a lemon, the Earth – a fly*
*Before the day ends you shall arrive*

## The Milky Way

Oh, Milky Way! You, whom the poet Apollinaire
	saw
as the shining sister of those in love:
streams of your stars, like lovers' naked bodies,
flow away and disappear into the fogs of the
	universe.

What flows away from me is your immense
	profuseness.
I've read that if your stars were grains of rice,
they would fill a cathedral. When freed, they would
	spread
from our Earth up to the Moon. How can we grasp
	this? – How?!

*Josef Tomáš*

## The afterglow

Oh –, a little oh –, a muffled oh –, an oh –
fading away into silence … Then I, too,
may fade away and be fully imbued
with that in which everything wholly dwells.

Nothing, absolutely nothing here is
as it seems. Even faith and love and hope
are empty words, if they are not imbued
with that in which everything wholly dwells.

# Paul Davies

Paul Davies is a British-born theoretical physicist, cosmologist, astrobiologist and best-selling author. He held academic appointments at the Universities of Cambridge, London and Newcastle upon Tyne until 1990, when he moved to Australia to take up the position as Professor of Mathematical Physics at The University of Adelaide, and later as Professor of Natural Philosophy at Macquarie University in Sydney, where he helped establish the NASA-affiliated Australian Centre for Astrobiology. He joined Arizona State University as the director of *Beyond*, a research centre devoted to exploring the "big questions" of science, such as how the universe began, the possibility of time travel and whether there is life beyond Earth. He is known for his work on black holes and for his explanation of the enigmatic "ripples" in the fading afterglow of the big bang. He is also one of the first to champion the idea that life may have come to Earth from Mars.

Paul Davies has written or co-authored 27 books, most recently *Cosmic Jackpot: Why our universe is just right for life* (published under the title *The Goldilocks*

*Enigma* in the UK). He writes regularly for newspapers, journals and magazines in several countries, and has made numerous radio and television documentaries in the UK and Australia. In 1995, he was awarded the Templeton Prize for his work on the deeper meaning of science. He has also been awarded the Faraday Prize by The Royal Society and the Kelvin Medal by the UK Institute of Physics. In June 2007, he was named a Member of the Order of Australia in the Queen's birthday honours list. And finally, on an astronomical note, the asteroid 1992 OG was renamed (6870) *Pauldavies* in recognition of his work on cosmic impacts.

# Virginia MacKenny

Virginia MacKenny is a practising artist and Senior Lecturer in Painting at the Michaelis School of Fine Art at the University of Cape Town. She has received a number of awards, including the Volkskas Atelier Award (1991) and the Ampersand Fellowship in New York (2004). She is an independent critic and curator. In 2006, she co-curated with Gabi Ngcobo *Second to None,* an exhibition for the Iziko South African National Gallery, celebrating the 50th anniversary of the 1956 Women's March on Pretoria to protest the apartheid Pass Laws Act. She supports contemporary visual arts discourse in South Africa by writing for *ArtSA* (www.artthrob.co.za) and *Nka*, and was an invited writer for Sophie Perryer's *10 Years 100 Artists – Art in a Democratic South Africa* (2004 She recently exhibited *Foam Along the Waterline* (2008), an exhibition of paintings and etchings at the Irma Stern Museum, Cape Town.

# Josef Tomáš

Josef Tomáš is a Czech-born mechanical engineer whose hobby is poetry. He received his engineering degree at the Czech Technical University in Prague in 1957 and his Ph.D. at the Czech Academy of Sciences in 1966. After the Soviet invasion of his home country in 1968, he immigrated to Germany, where he worked at the Volkswagen Research Centre in Wolfsburg. In 1976, he accepted an academic position at RMIT in Melbourne, Australia, where he worked until 1994. He then founded a private firm involved in R&D for the automotive industry, where he is still active.

In regard to poetry, he wrote in one of his Czech books: *"What was I supposed to write to my mother, when I knew that my letters were being opened and read by the Czech secrete police. So, somehow all by itself, my recollection of her, of my home and of my youth began to take a verse form."* After the collapse of communism in Czechoslovakia, he published some of his books, first for his closest friends, then for a wider readership.

The *World in My Mouth* is the first translation of a collection of his own poems, inspired by reading the books of Dr. Paul Davies, a theoretical physicist he admires very much.


**Books in Czech:**
Six books of poetry

**English translations of Czech poets (published by Arima Publishing, UK):**
Vladimír Holan, *The First Testament* (including *A Dream*), 2005
Vladimír Holan, *Soliloquy with Shakespeare* (*A Night with Hamlet* and *A Night with Ophelia*), 2007
Jiří Orten, *Selected Poems*, 2007
Vladimír Holan, *Narrative Poems I*, 2008
Vladimír Holan, *Narrative Poems II*, 2009

www.ingramcontent.com/pod-product-compliance
Lightning Source LLC
Chambersburg PA
CBHW020023050426
42450CB00005B/613